UK employment

Redundancy

Bullet Points

email: robin@worklaw.co.uk
website: www.worklaw.co.uk
telephone: 07549 168 675

© Robin Hawker
All rights reserved
May 2020

ISBN: 9798640617481
Imprint: Independently published

UK Employment Law

Bullet Point Booklets

1. Disciplinary Procedures
2. National Minimum Wage
3. Employment Contracts
4. Defending Employment Tribunal Claims
5. TUPE
6. Staff Handbooks
7. Disability Discrimination
8. Settlement Agreements
9. This booklet

Disclaimer

This series of booklets is titled *UK employment law*. This is not an entirely accurate title. The focus is on the law of England and Wales. Employment laws in Scotland and Northern Ireland are broadly the same as in England and Wales but may differ occasionally.

Employment law is complex and changes frequently due to political, social and economic pressures, and the law might have changed by the time you read this booklet: the publication date is on the title page.

Please view this booklet as a brief, *bullet-pointed* guide to employment law. It is not a complete guide. You must not rely on this booklet for anything other than a brief overview of the law and procedures: our attempt to simplify the law might cause misunderstanding and ambiguities.

This booklet does not—and cannot—cover everything. For example, where bullet-point lists are given they may be incomplete as only more common items might be listed.

You are advised to consult a specialist in employment law (https://worklaw.co.uk) to answer specific questions.

Index

Redundancy	1 - 4
An unfair redundancy	5
A fair redundancy	6
Avoiding redundancies	7
A redundancy plan	8 - 10
A redundancy procedure	11
Redundancy situation	12
Redundancy policy	13 - 16
Redundancy consultations	17 - 22
Electing employee representatives	21 - 27
Alternatives to redundancy	28 - 29
A pool of candidates	30
Selection	31 - 33
Employee Rights	34 - 36
Leaving voluntarily	37
Early retirement	38
Flexible working	39
Lay-offs & short-time working	40 - 42
Bumping	43 - 45
Notice	46
Appeals	47

REDUNDANCY

Simple definitions of 'redundancy'

The UK government website defines redundancy as *'when an employer dismisses an employee because the employer no longer needs anyone to do the employee's job, because, for example, the business is changing what it does, doing things in a different way, or closing down'*. The website then says that for a redundancy to be genuine the employer must demonstrate that the employee's job will no longer exist.

In its booklet entitled 'Handling small-scale redundancies', Acas defines 'redundancy' as *'where an employer needs to reduce their workforce - for example, if the business is closing or certain work is no longer required'*.

The above definitions of 'redundancy' are simple and easy to understand. However, neither is a complete definition.

The complete definition of 'redundancy', and the definition which will be relevant in the event of a case in an employment tribunal, is set out in the next paragraph.

Complete definition of redundancy

Two questions of fact need to be answered to define *redundancy*:

- has the employer's requirement for employees to carry out work of *a particular kind* ceased or diminished?
- if so, is a dismissal for redundancy attributable, wholly or mainly, to that cessation or diminution?

The first question is to do with the state of the business.

The second question is one of causation.

There is a redundancy when the requirement for the number of *employees* doing *a particular kind* of work has ceased or diminished, or is expected to do so.

The emphasis is on *a particular kind*.

The *particular kind of work* is not restricted to what work is required to be performed under the employment contract.

There is no reason in law why the dismissal of an employee should not be *attributable to*, or caused by, a diminution in the employer's need for *employees* irrespective of the terms of the employee's employment contract or the job they did.

It is necessary to determine whether there is a diminution in the requirement for *employees* (not necessarily the dismissed employee) to carry out work of a particular kind.

The definition we give in this paragraph is not simple to understand. In particular, it is not easy to understand what the words, *a particular kind of work*, mean in in the context of a redundancy. But please see the example below.

Example of the complete definition

There were two fork-lift drivers delivering materials to two factory machines. Each of the two machines had an operator. The employer decided that it needed only one machine instead of two, which meant that it did not need one of the machine operators. The employer then decided to make one of the machine operators into a fork-lift driver. This meant that the employer now had three drivers (the 2 original drivers plus the former machine-operator) but only needed two drivers. After following a fair redundancy procedure, the employers dismissed one of the original drivers, not the former machine operator. Is there still a redundancy? The answer is 'yes'. Although the employer required the same number of drivers (two), and the dismissed employee was a driver, there had been a diminution in the requirement to carry out the work of a machine-operator (a particular kind of work) and this diminution had caused the driver's dismissal. The dismissal was *attributable* to the fact that the requirement for the number of employees (the machine operators) doing a *particular kind* of work (operating the machines) has ceased or diminished (one required instead of 2), and there was a redundancy situation.

Case law
The complete definition of redundancy, we have given above, is derived from case-law.
By 'case-law' we mean judgments in cases which interpret the legal effect of the wording in relevant legislation laid down by Parliament when the wording is unclear or fails to cover the point in dispute: that judgment then clarifies and becomes part of the law.

Three points to note
(1) The termination of employment, because of redundancy, is a dismissal.
(2) The above example presupposes that the employer has gone through a fair redundancy procedure before arriving at a decision

to dismiss for redundancy otherwise the employee who is made redundant would have an arguable claim for unfair dismissal (assuming that they had the required length of service to make a claim).

(3) The above example is also one of *bumping* (see the section called **Bumping**).

An unfair redundancy

A dismissal by reason of redundancy can be unfair for one of 3 reasons:

- there was no true redundancy situation (see the definition of **Redundancy**);
- there was a true redundancy situation, but a failure by the employer to consult properly with **employees affected** by the dismissal, or a failure to consult *collectively* if 20 or more employees are proposed to be dismissed within a 90-day period (see **Redundancy consultations**).
- there was an unfair selection procedure (see **A fair redundancy**);
- the employer failed to consider suitable **alternative employment**.

Employees affected

The obligation on the employer to to consult is with *employees affected* by the proposed redundancies. This includes employees who may not be made redundant but who may be affected by the redundancies because, for example, their workload increases as there will be fewer employees to do the work following redundancies.

A fair redundancy

If a claim is made in an employment tribunal, that a redundancy was unfair, the tribunal will consider 3 points of law:

- the first point is whether there was a true redundancy situation (see the definition of **Redundancy**);
- the second point is whether whether a redundancy dismissal lay within *the range of conduct* which a reasonable employer could have adopted;
- the third point is whether the employer acted *reasonably* in treating redundancy *as a sufficient reason for dismissing the employee.*

If the circumstances of the employer make it inevitable that some employees must be dismissed for redundancy, it is still necessary for the employment tribunal to consider the means whereby the applicant was selected to be the employee to be dismissed and the reasonableness of the steps taken by the employer to choose the applicant, rather than some other employee, for dismissal.

Avoiding redundancies

Within reason, an employer is entitled to run their business as they see fit, even though they might run the business unwisely. However, in the interests of good industrial relations, and the economy in general, and the reputation of the business, an employer should always try to avoid redundancies whenever possible.

Possible steps to avoid redundancies include:

- seeking applicants for *voluntary* redundancy or early retirement;
- seeking applications from existing staff to work flexibly;
- temporarily reducing working hours;
- retraining employees to do other jobs which are needed;
- laying off self-employed contractors, freelancers or non-employees;
- not using casual labour;
- not recruiting new employees, unless their specialisation is needed;
- reducing or stopping overtime;
- filling vacancies elsewhere in the business with existing employees;
- encouraging employees to take 'career breaks' or sabbaticals;
- salary sacrifice arrangements;
- making **a redundancy plan** (see next section).

A redundancy plan

An employer, who identifies the need for redundancies, should plan how to:

- consult staff about the potential redundancy;
- try and avoid compulsory redundancies;
- devise and implement a redundancy procedure;
- give staff notice;
- work out redundancy pay;
- support remaining staff;
- plan for the future.

If there is a recognised trade union in the business, the employer should consult with the trade union concerned as to the possibility of redundancies.

If there is no recognised trade union in the business with which to consult, the employer should consider consulting with employee representatives.

As we shall see in the section headed **Redundancy consultations**, if the employer is contemplating making 20 or more employees redundant in a period of 90 days or less, unless there is a recognised trade union, it is necessary for the employer to arrange for the election of employee representatives and then consult with the elected employee representatives before any redundancies take place.

Persons affected by a redundancy situation

Once employees become aware of a redundancy situation this can

have an unsettling and worrying affect on all concerned. Employers should consider how best to support:
- those employees at risk of redundancy;
- those managing the redundancy process;
- those involved in consultation process;
- employee representatives;
- employees who are then made redundant;
- employees who are not made redundant but who may be adversely affected by the redundancy process.

Employees who are not made redundant might still suffer stress from seeing colleagues and friends being made redundant, and worry that they will be made redundant in the future. Employers should consider giving support by:
- counselling;
- help with advice about personal finances;
- disclosing plans for the business;
- retraining employees for more job security;
- If necessary, helping the employee find alternative employment.

Managers who are delegated to deal with impending redundancies should:
- know why the proposed redundancies are necessary;
- be trained or tutored in how best to deal with the redundancy procedure;
- be able to give sufficient time to carry out the redundancy procedure properly;

- know who they can turn to for support themselves.

If the situation is handled in the right way it can make a big difference to:
- how staff react and cope with being made redundant;
- the morale of staff who are staying on;
- the success of the planned changes and future of the business.

Jobcentre Plus

Employers should also contact and co-operate with Jobcentre Plus in helping redundant employees into another job.

Employers can also help redundant employees write or update CVs.

A redundancy procedure

Once the employer identifies that redundancies might be needed the employer should:

- ensure that there is a genuine **redundancy situation**;
- implement a written **redundancy policy**, existing or new;
- enter into **redundancy consultations**;
- consider **alternatives** to redundancies;
- identify a '**pool**' of candidates for redundancy;
- implement a fair **selection** criteria;
- give employees their redundancy **rights**.

Redundancy situations

The expression 'redundancy situation' is not defined in employment law but is generally accepted to mean that the employer needs to:

- reduce staff numbers; or
- close the business entirely; or
- close a place of work, but not the whole business.

And it is always necessary to consider the definition of **redundancy** we have set out in the first section of this booklet.

Redundancy policy

It is not mandatory for an employer to have a written redundancy policy, but is makes a redundancy procedure simpler and more efficient if one is drafted once the possibility of redundancies is identified.

It may be that the business already has a written redundancy policy as a stand-alone document, or as part of another document such as a staff handbook. If so, a copy of the redundancy policy can be given to employees, or they can be reminded where their copy of the policy may be found, such as in the staff handbook.

Very occasionally, a redundancy policy and procedure is referred to, or included in, an employment contract, in which case, the redundancy policy is likely to be contractual.

It is unwise to have a redundancy policy and procedure which is contractual because, unless the employer follows the procedure exactly as written, there is a risk that the employer will face a claim of breach of contract for failing to follow the policy.

Below is a simple redundancy policy which is not designed for any particular type of business, but which covers all of the main points in a redundancy procedure which may need to be covered.

Draft redundancy policy
REDUNDANCY POLICY
1. ABOUT THIS POLICY
1.1 We will always try to avoid the need for compulsory redundancies but sometimes these may be necessary. The pattern or volume of our business or methods of working may change and

requirements for employees may reduce.

1.2 The purpose of this policy is to ensure that, whenever reduction in employee numbers may become necessary:

(a) we communicate clearly with all affected employees and ensure that they are treated fairly;

(b) we try to find ways of avoiding compulsory redundancies;

(c) we consult with employees; and

(d) any selection for compulsory redundancy is undertaken fairly, reasonably and without discrimination.

1.3 This policy applies to all employees. It does not apply to agency workers, consultants or self-employed contractors.

1.4 This policy will be reviewed from time to time to ensure that it reflects our legal obligations and our business needs.

1.5 This policy does not form part of any employee's contract of employment and we may amend it at any time.

2. AVOIDING COMPULSORY REDUNDANCIES

2.1 Where we are proposing to make redundancies we will enter into consultation with all affected employees on an individual basis and, where appropriate, also with recognised trade unions and/or employee representatives.

2.2 In the first instance we will consider steps that might, depending on the circumstances, be taken to avoid the need for compulsory redundancies. Examples of such steps include:

(a) Reviewing the use of agency staff, self-employed contractors and consultants.

(b) Restricting recruitment in affected categories of employee and in those areas into which affected employees might be redeployed.

(c) Reducing overtime in affected departments to that needed to meet contractual commitments or provide essential services.

(d) Freezing salaries for a specified period.

(e) Considering the introduction of short-time working, job-sharing or other flexible working arrangements, where these are practicable.

(f) Identifying suitable alternative work with us or with any other companies within the Group that might be offered to potentially redundant employees.

(g) Inviting applications for early retirement or voluntary redundancy. In all cases the acceptance of a volunteer for redundancy will be a matter of our discretion and we reserve the right not to offer voluntary redundancy terms or to refuse an application where it is not in the interests of our business to do so.

2.3 Any measures adopted must not adversely affect our business and our ability to serve our customers.

3. MAKING COMPULSORY REDUNDANCIES

3.1 When it is not possible to avoid making compulsory redundancies, we will advise all affected employees and, where appropriate, recognised trade unions and/or employee representatives, that compulsory redundancies cannot be avoided. We will consult on the procedure that will then be followed and the criteria that will be applied.

3.2 In carrying out any redundancy exercise we will not discriminate directly or indirectly on grounds of gender, sexual orientation, marital or civil partner status, gender reassignment, race, colour, nationality, ethnic or national origin, religion or belief, disability or age. Part-time employees and those working under fixed-term contracts will not be treated differently to permanent, full-time comparators.

3.3 The criteria used to select those employees who will potentially be made redundant will be objective, transparent and fair and based on the skills required to meet our existing and anticipated business needs.

3.4 We will then consult individually with those employees who have been provisionally selected for redundancy.

3.5 Where selection for redundancy is confirmed, employees selected for redundancy will be given notice of termination of employment in accordance with their contracts and written confirmation of the payments that they will receive. Employees will be given the opportunity to appeal against this decision.

3.6 We will continue to look for alternative employment for redundant employees and inform them of any vacancies that we have until their termination dates. The manner in which redundant employees will be invited to apply for and be interviewed for vacancies will be organised depending on the circumstances existing at the time. Alternative employment may be offered subject to a trial period where appropriate.

3.7 Where we are unable to offer alternative employment we will assist employees to look for work with other employers. Employees under notice of redundancy may be entitled to take a reasonable amount of paid time off work to look for alternative employment or to arrange training for future employment.

Redundancy consultations

If an employer does not consult employees in a redundancy situation, any redundancies they make will almost certainly be unfair and result in a loss in an employment tribunal. And if 20 or more employees are to be made redundant there is a mandatory obligation on the employer to consult.

Mandatory consultation

It is mandatory for an employer to follow *collective consultation* rules if they are making 20 or more employees redundant within any 90-day period or less at a single establishment.

In simple terms, an *establishment* is the site where an employee is assigned to work (but there is case law on the point and an employer may need to take professional advice as to whether, in their case, there is an establishment).

If the above applies the employer will need to complete an HR1 form. There are heavy financial penalties, and it is a criminal offence, for failure to do so.

An HR1 form

Employers are strongly advised to download an HR1 form from the following government website: https://www.gov.uk/government/publications/redundancy-payments-form-hr1-advance-notification-of-redundancies (or Google "redundancy HR1 form").

The form is in PDF and ODT formats and consists of 2 pages.

If you cannot obtain a copy of the form then we outline the main points on the form as below.

The HR1 form is produced by The Insolvency Service.

Under the heading *Note for employer* the form says:
There is a statutory requirement for the Government to assist employees facing redundancy. In order to do this, advance notification of potential redundancies is required from you. Failure to comply with the statutory notification requirements below without good cause may result in prosecution and a fine, on summary conviction, for the company and/or officer of the company. The Redundancy Payments Service (RPS), acting on behalf of the Secretary of State for Business, Innovation and Skills, collects the information and distributes it to the appropriate Government Departments and Agencies who offer job brokering services and/or training services so that they can discharge their obligation to your employees. The information about your company is commercially confidential and may be used only for the purpose of assisting those facing redundancy. The other Government Departments and Agencies are bound by the same confidentiality terms as the RPS. You will be contacted directly by your local Jobcentre Plus and other service providers in your local area with offers of assistance during this notification/consultation period.

The next paragraph is *How to complete this form* and where to send it. The next paragraph is headed *Further information on assistance for employers* and says where more copies of the form may be obtained. The next paragraph is headed *Your legal obligations*. It says, what we have said above, which is that employers are required by law to notify the Redundancy Payments Service (RPS) of a proposal to dismiss 20 or more employees as redundant at one establishment within a period of 90 days or less.

- An HR1 form must be completed for each establishment (site) where 20 or more redundancies are proposed.
- *The minimum period* for notification and consultation for between 20 to 99 redundancies at one establishment (site) *is at least 30 days before the first dismissal.*
- If there are to be 100 or more redundancies at one establishment (site) the minimum period for notification and consultation is 45 days.
- An employer must notify the RPS at least 30 days (or 45 days if 100 redundancies proposed) before the first dismissal and before the employer issues any individual notices of dismissal.
- The employer must send a copy of the HR1 form to the representatives of the employees being consulted (a recognised trade union or elected employee representatives).
- The paragraph explains why the employer should do if further redundancies are needed following submission of the HR1 form.
- The date the employer is deemed to have notified the RPS is the date on which the RPS receives the form.
- If it is not reasonable practical for the employer to comply with the minimum notification periods (30 days or 45 days as above) the form emphasises that the employer must give

reasons why they did not provide the information on time. The next paragraphs are numbered 1 to 11.

Paragraphs 1 and 2 ask for the employer's details and contact details.

Paragraph 3 ask for the addresses of the establishment(s) where redundancies are proposed.

Paragraph 4 which is headed *Timing of redundancies* ask for the date of the first proposed dismissal and the date of the last proposed dismissal. And under 4(c) asks for the reason for late notification if the employer has given less than the 30 (or 45) days notice required.

Paragraph 5 is headed *Method of selection for redundancy* with very little space on the form to explain the method (we suggest attaching a copy of the relevant Redundancy Policy).

Paragraph 6 is headed *Staff numbers/redundancies at this establishment* and lists 8 occupational groups and asks for the total number of employees in the group and the number of possible redundancies in that group.

Paragraph 7 is headed *Nature of main business (SIC code)*. The SIC code is a five-digit Standard Industrial Classification code for providing Companies House with a description of the business and is only relevant for businesses which are limited companies. If the employer is not a limited company that should say what their business is.

Paragraph 8 is headed *Closure of the business* and asks if the employer proposes to close the establishment (site).

Paragraph 9 is headed *Reasons for redundancies* and asks the employer to tick one of more of 7 boxes to show the reasons for the proposed redundancies, with a brief space for the details. *Paragraph 10* is headed *Consultation* and ask for the name of the recognised trade union with which the employer is consulting or the names of elected employee representatives if there is no recognised trade union. *Paragraph 10 c)* asks whether the employer has given a copy of the HR1 form to the trade union or elected employee representatives. *Paragraph 10 d)* asks whether the consolation process has started, with dates. *Paragraph 10 f)* asks whether the employer has given individual notices of dismissal. *Paragraph 11* is headed *Declaration* which the employer has to sign to confirm that the contents of the form are true.

Points to note
(1) It is evident from *paragraph 10* that the employer needs to have embarked of a consultation process before being able to complete the HR1 form.
(2) Consultation does not have to end in agreement, but it must be carried out with a view to reaching it, including ways of avoiding or reducing the redundancies.
(3) There is no time limit on how long consultations last but there is a minimum period before an employer can dismiss any employees (either 30 or 45 days).
(4) The trade union or elected employee representatives (jointly referred to as 'the representatives') must be given enough time to consider the employer's redundancy proposals.
(5) the employer must give the representatives any further

information requested unless there are justifiable reasons as to why the information cannot be given.

Fewer than 20 redundancies

There are no set rules to follow if there are fewer than 20 redundancies planned, but it is good practice to consult fully employees and their representatives.

If a claim is made to an employment tribunal alleging that there was no true redundancy situation or that there was a flawed redundancy procedure, an employment tribunal is very likely to take into consideration whether or not the employer consulted with employees or their representatives before arriving at a decision to dismiss for redundancy, and may find that the dismissal was unfair in the absence of proper consultation.

The best policy is for an employer to proceed, more or less, as they would do if obligated to submit an HR1 form.

In any event an employer should always:

- consult with employees or their representatives
- consider how best to avoid or minimise redundancies
- implement a fair redundancy policy.

The requirement to consider how best to avoid or minimise redundancies, includes considering alternative employment, not only in the company which employs the redundant employees but also in any other company or business which could reasonably be said to be in the same group of businesses.

Electing employee representatives

An employer will need to arrange for the election of *employee representatives* with whom to consult regarding the proposed redundancies in the event that the employer proposes to make *20 or more employees redundant in a period of 90 days or less* and there is *no* **recognised trade union** in the workplace.

The arrangement for the election should mimic, in so far as is possible, a political election such as a general election to elect a UK government or the local election of a counsellor.

The employer must consult with employee representatives with the aim of reaching agreement.

An employer who fails to consult may have to pay a **penalty**.

Penalty

When an employer fails to consult, when they are required by law to do so, they may have to pay a *protective award*.

A protective award requires employers to pay employees their normal week's pay for a period of time called the *protected period*.

The tribunal has the discretion in fixing the length of the protected period, depending upon what is just and equitable and taking account of the seriousness of the employer's default.

The maximum length of the protected period is 90 days in all cases where 20 or more are to be made redundant.

A failure on the part of the employer, to comply with mandatory election obligations, could be very, very expensive.

Is an election necessary?

An election of employee representative will not be necessary if there is a recognised trade union in the workplace.

Also, an election will not be necessary is the employee have elected representatives already, for another purpose, such as with regard to pensions or a TUPE transfer.

Collective redundancies

The obligation in is to inform and consult appropriate representatives of affected employees. The affected employees are those who may be affected by the proposed collective redundancies. This is wider than just those employees who may be at risk of dismissal. For example, it would include those employees who will not be dismissed but whose workloads will change as a result of the dismissals of colleagues.

Recognised trade union

If the employer recognises a trade union in respect of all the affected employees, the appropriate representatives are trade union representatives. This covers all those employees affected by the proposed redundancies: it is irrelevant whether they are union members or not.

Recognised means that the employer recognises the union to any extent for the purposes of collective bargaining, which means *negotiations related to or connected with* one or more of the following:

- terms and conditions of employment;

- or working conditions;
- engagement, termination or suspension of employment;
- allocation of work or duties;
- matters of discipline;
- membership of a trade union;
- facilities for trade unions officials;
- consultation procedures relating to any of the above;
- An employer with a recognised trade union must therefore consult with the trade union representatives in respect of affected employees.

The employer cannot choose to consult with other representatives of those employees.

Partly-unionised

Sometimes an employer may recognise a union in respect of only some of the affected employees. But it is irrelevant whether individual employees are union members or not: in other words, whether they are members of the *bargaining unit*. What matters is whether they are in the bargaining unit.

Where there are affected employees outside the bargaining unit, the employer will have to inform and consult union representatives, or elected representatives, in respect of those employees.

Existing employee representatives

For affected employees in respect of whom no union is recognised (even if they are members of a union), there might already be representatives with authority to consult on their behalf. For example, employees representatives might have been elected because of TUPE. If this is the case, the employer can choose to deal with the exiting representatives or to arrange for the election of new representatives.

Individual consultation

If there is no trade union and no existing employee representatives, the employer has a duty to arrange elections. The employer cannot consult with employees directly if it has not first given employees a chance to elect representatives.

If the employees choose not to elect representatives, or fail to do so, the employer must still consult with them individually.

Election procedure

There is no election procedure which must be followed by law: the obligation on an employer is to arrange an election procedure which is fair and reasonable in the circumstances.

However, there are some pointers as to what an employment tribunal would consider fair and reasonable, as follows:

- the employer must invite employees to elect representatives in sufficient time to begin consultation;
- any employee who is a candidate to be elected as an employee representative should be someone *affected* by the proposed redundancies;
- the employer must decide how many employee

representatives should be elected;
- there must be sufficient representatives to represent the interests of all affected employees,
- all employees affected by the proposed redundancies must be entitled to vote;
- voting should be secret;
- all votes must be counted.

The above is not a complete list of all factors which might be relevant.

Fail to elect representatives

If employees have been asked to elect employee representatives but fail to do so, the employer will be deemed to have complied with its obligations to consult about the proposed redundancies if it gives the necessary information direct to the *affected* employees.

Alternatives to redundancy

An employer is obliged to consider possible alternatives to making employees redundant. In particular, whether there is **alternative employment** for a candidate or candidates for redundancy.

Please also refer to the section: **Avoiding redundancies**.

Alternative employment

An employer is obliged to offer a candidate for redundancy *suitable alternative employment* within the employer's business or an associated business: a failure to do so could amount to an unfair dismissal. Whether a job is *suitable* depends on factors such as:

- how similar the work is to the redundant job;
- the terms of the job being offered;
- the employee's skills, abilities and circumstances in relation to the job;
- the pay (including benefits);
- job status;
- hours;
- place of work.

If the employee *unreasonably* refuses an offer of suitable alternative employment they may lose their right to statutory redundancy pay. An employee, offered alternative employment, has the right to a 4 week trial period to see whether the alternative job offered is suitable.

The 4 week period may be extended if the employee needs training to do the job being offered, provided any extension is agreed in writing with the employer before the trial period commences. The employee must tell the employer during the trial period if they decide the new job is not suitable for them. In which case, the employee will still be entitled to statutory redundancy pay.

Associated business

It is important to consider what 'associated' means in the context of redundancies.

The legislation refers to an associated *company* meaning a limited company, in the same group.

However, it is probably wise for an employer, with a business which is not a limited company, when considering the availability of alternative employment, to include any other business which is effectively controlled by the same employer and can reasonably be said to be associated.

A pool of candidates

An employer's first step when approaching a redundancy selection should be to identify the *pool of employees* from which those who are to be made redundant will be selected, as whether the employer identified a fair pool will be considered by an employment tribunal when assessing the fairness of the dismissal.

If an employer simply dismisses an employee without first properly identifying a pool, the dismissal is likely to be unfair, regardless of the fair selection criteria applied.

If in doubt as to whether a particular job role should be included in the pool it is best to include it.

Fair selection criteria

Fair reasons for selecting employees for redundancy could include:
- skills, qualifications and aptitude;
- standard of work and/or performance;
- attendance (unless affected by a disability);
- disciplinary record.

As far as possible, *objective* (not subjective) selection criteria, precisely defined and capable of being applied in an independent way should be used when determining which employees are to be selected for redundancy.

An employment tribunal will ask whether the selection for redundancy was one which a reasonable employer could have made, taking into account the size and administrative resources of the employer's business.

It may be that no selection criteria is necessary, for example, when the employer is closing its business and all employees are going to be redundant

Unfair selection criteria

Some selection criteria are automatically unfair. An employer must not select an employee for redundancy based on any of the following reasons (the list is not exhaustive):
- pregnancy, including all reasons relating to maternity
- family, including parental leave, paternity leave (birth and adoption), adoption leave or time off for dependants
- acting as an employee representative

- acting as a trade union representative
- joining or not joining a trade union
- being a part-time or fixed-term employee
- age, disability, gender reassignment, marriage and civil partnership, religion or belief, sex and sexual orientation
- pay and working hours, including the Working Time Regulations, annual leave and the National Minimum Wage.

Selection methods

In general terms, employers must give as much warning as possible of impending redundancies to any affected employee.

Where there is a recognised trade union in the business:

- employers must consult the union on the redundancy procedure and seek to agree with the union the criteria to be applied in selecting the employees to be made redundant;
- whether or not an agreement as to the criteria to be adopted has been reached with the union, employers should seek to establish criteria for selection which, so far as possible, do not depend solely upon the opinion of the person making the selection but can be objectively checked against such things as attendance record, efficiency at the job, experience, or length of service;
- selection must be made fairly in accordance with these criteria and employers should consider any representations the union may make as to such selection;

- employers must seek to establish whether, instead of dismissing an employee, the employer could offer alternative employment.

Where there is no recognised trade union, and employee should consult with employees either individuals or collectively or both individually and collectively (see **Redundancy consultations**) and proceed, in so far as is possible, as if they were dealing with a trade union.

Points to note

(1) An employer can select employees for redundancy employees on a *last in - first out* basis, but only if they can justify using this criterion.

(2) It is unwise for employers to use *length of service* as the only selection criterion as this might be age discrimination.

(3) Regular absence from work can be an important criterion, but employers should be careful to enquire about the reason behind the absence; it might be that the absence was caused by a disability in which case there is a risk of a disability discrimination claim, or a sex discrimination claim if the absence was because of pregnancy.

(4) Employees on maternity leave who are made redundant during either their ordinary or additional maternity leave have the right to be offered any suitable alternative employment in preference to other employees (further consideration of maternity rights is beyond the scope of this booklet).

Employee rights

When redundancy is contemplated, employees have rights as follows:

- a right to reasonable **time off** to look for a new job or arrange training;
- a right not to be selected for redundancy unfairly (this will be an **unfair dismissal**);
- a right to **redundancy pay**, if they qualify.

Time off

Employers must allow employees a reasonable amount of time off to look for another job or training if:

- they are being made redundant;
- they have worked continuously for the employer for at least 2 years.Paying staff who take time off to look for another job
- pay employees who take time off to look for alternative work up to 40% of one week's pay (this is the total amount and not the amount per week).

Unfair dismissal

Redundancy is a potentially fair reason for dismissal but it will be for the employer to prove that redundancy was the principal reason for the dismissal.

If an employee is unfairly selected for redundancy this will amount to an unfair dismissal.

The employee will qualify to claim unfair dismissal if they have been employed continuously by the employer for at least 2 years (including any employment to which TUPE applies)

Unfair dismissal claims will involve consideration of the substantive fairness of the reason for the dismissal and the procedural fairness of the employer's actions when handling the dismissal.

Even if the reason for the dismissal was redundancy, however, the dismissal can still be unfair if the employer did not act reasonably in dismissing the employee. In deciding whether a dismissal was fair, an employment tribunal will look at issues such as:

- consultation;
- selection;
- alternative employment.

Redundancy pay

An employee will qualify for *statutory* redundancy pay if:

- they have been employed continually by the employer (including under TUPE) for at least 2 years; and
- have been dismissed, laid off or put on short-time working.

An employee might be entitled to enhanced redundancy pay, beyond statutory redundancy pay, under their contract of employment: in other words, *contractual* redundancy pay. Or the employer might give enhanced redundancy pay on a *discretionary* basis.

Statutory redundancy pay rates

Statutory redundancy pay is based on an employee's age and length of employment, calculating backwards from the dismissal date. The rates change from year to year, usually in April, but are calculated as follows:

- half a week's pay for each full year under 22;
- one week's pay for each full year 22 or older, but under 41;
- one and half week's pay for each full year 41 or older.

On or after 6 April 2020, weekly pay is capped at £538. This figure is likely to increase slightly in April 2021.

The length of service is capped at 20 years.

The maximum statutory redundancy pay would be £16,140 (£538 x 1.5 weeks x 20 years).

Claim for redundancy pay

Its the employer does not pay all of the redundancy pay due to an employee, the employee has a right to make a claim for payment to an employment tribunal.

The time limit for making a claim to an employment tribunal for statutory redundancy pay is 6 months less one day from the date of the employee's dismissal.

If the employer does not pay because it is insolvent the employee may be able to make a limited claim against the National Insurance Fund.

(Insolvency and the National Insurance Fund are beyond the scope of this booklet).

Leaving voluntarily

In the section **Avoiding redundancies** we said that one of the ways to try and avoid making making redundancies, or fewer redundancies, is to ask some employees to take *voluntary* redundancy or early retirement. However:

- the employer must have a fair and transparent selection procedure before making anyone redundant;
- the employer must tell employees they will not automatically be selected for redundancy just because they volunteered for redundancy;
- employers should also make clear that early retirement is not automatically given.

An employer can offer extra redundancy pay if they want to encourage employees to volunteer.

Points to note

(1) Employees who have volunteered to be made redundant should be included in the total to see whether 20 or more employees are to made redundant within 90 days, in which event the employer must consult collectively with a recognised trade union or elected employee representatives.

Early retirement

In the section **Avoiding redundancies** we said that one of the ways to try and avoid making making redundancies, or fewer redundancies, is to ask employees to take early retirement. However:

- an offer of early retirement must be made across the entire workforce;
- specific employees should not be singled out;
- an employer cannot force an employee to take early retirement; it must be the employee's choice, otherwise there could be a claim of unfair dismissal;
- an employer could be accused of age discrimination if they offer early retirement only to older employees.

It is possible for an employer to give incentives to employees to encourage them to retire early.

Flexible working

In the section **Avoiding redundancies** we said that one of the ways to try and avoid making making redundancies, or fewer redundancies, is to ask some employees to work flexibly. Flexible working could include:

- working fewer hours;
- homeworking;
- job sharing;
- working compressed hours;
- temporarily reducing hours.

Points to note

(1) Probably it will be necessary to vary employment contracts by agreement to allow for flexible working.

(2) Employees have a *statutory* right to request flexible working once they meet certain conditions (a consideration of this statutory right is beyond the scope of this booklet).

Lay-offs and short-time working

A right to *lay-off* employees or place them on *short-time working* must be included in the employment contract otherwise the employee does not have the right to lay-off employees or place them on short-time working.

A *lay-off* happens when an employer does not have sufficient work for an employee and asks that employee not to come into work for at least one working day.

Short-Time working is when an employee works reduced hours or is paid less than half a week's pay.

Laying off staff or short-time working can help avoid redundancies - but employers should agree this with employees first.

Contractual right necessary

In the absence of a clause in the employment contract entitling an employer to lay off employees or place them on short-time working and reduce their wages accordingly, to do either would be a breach of the employment contract and would amount to an *unlawful deductions of wages*.

Application for redundancy

There is no time limit, as such, as to how long an employee can be laid off or put on short-time working.

However, once the employee has been laid off or on short-time working for 4 weeks in a row, or 6 weeks in a 13-week period, they can apply for redundancy, and a statutory redundancy payment if

they have been employed by the employer for 2 years or more.
The employer has 7 days to accept a redundancy claim or give the employee a written counter-notice.

A counter-notice means the employer expects available work will start within 4 weeks and will last at least 13 weeks.

The employee must resign to get redundancy pay. They have 3 weeks to hand in their notice, starting from 7 days after they gave written notice to their employer unless the employer served a counter-notice.

Guarantee pay

If an employee is laid off or placed on short-time working, and the employment contracts permits this, the employee is entitled to claim *guarantee pay*.

The maximum amount of guarantee pay is £30 a day for 5 days in any 3-month period which is a maximum of £150.

If the employee normally earns less than £30 a day the applicable guarantee will be the amount they earn a day.

Part-time employees are entitled to claim proportionately in line with the periods referred to above.

An employee cannot claim guarantee pay for any day on which they do some work.

Eligibility

In order to be eligible to claim guarantee pay the employee must:
- have been employed continuously for 1 month (includes

part-time workers);
- be available for work;
- not refuse any reasonable alternative work;
- not have been laid off because of industrial action.If it's included in employment contracts you can ask employees to:
  - stop working for a while (known as a 'temporary lay-off')
  - work fewer hours (known as 'short-time' working)

It must be a temporary solution and not a permanent change to agreed working hours.

If it's not included in employment contracts

You can ask to update an employee's contract to include these options. They do not have to accept.

Bumping

Bumping happens when, in the course of a redundancy procedure, an employee, whose job is redundant, ends up pushing (bumping) another employee out of their job, which is not redundant, so that the employee who occupies the non-redundant role is the one who is made redundant.

A common example of bumping is as follows. The role of a senior manager is redundant. The role of his junior manager is not redundant. The employer would like to keep the senior manager and offers the senior manager the junior manager's job The senior manager accepts the offer and the employer makes the junior manager redundant, even though the junior manager's job is not redundant?

The above example presupposes that the employer has gone through a fair redundancy procedure in respect of both employees before arriving at the decision to bump, otherwise the employee who is made redundant would have an arguable claim for unfair dismissal (assuming that they had the required length of service to make a claim).

Bumping could also apply in the case of 2 employees on the same level.

An employer should not assume that an employee, in a 'pool' of candidates for redundancy, would refuse a lesser role if one were offered. The employee should, at least, be given the opportunity to say 'yes' or 'no' to the lesser role. An employer's failure to consider bumping could give rise to an unfair dismissal claim.

Points on bumping

The starting point is that there is no obligation on an employer, to think of bumping as a way of saving the job of a candidate for redundancy. However, whether it is reasonable for the employer to have considered bumping will depend on the relevant factors in the particular case such as:

- whether bumping was a reasonable possibility
- the relevant differences between the 2 roles;
- the differences in remuneration between the 2 roles;
- the relative length of employment of the 2 employees;
- their respective qualifications and knowledge;
- any other relevant factors in the circumstances off the particular case.

Whether bumping is reasonable

As always, the issue to be considered in deciding whether a dismissal for redundancy was fair or unfair is whether what the employer decides about bumping is within *a band of reasonable responses* open to a reasonable employer.

A band of reasonable responses is a test which operates throughout employment law.

The duty of an employment tribunal, when considering a claim of unfair dismissal, is not to say what it would have done if it had been the employer, but to consider whether what the employer decided was within a range of possible decisions taken.

The advice is that bumping should be considered when looking at whether suitable alternative employment was available.

An employment tribunal might find, on the facts of the particular case, that bumping ought to have been considered, and that the employer's failure to do so might render the dismissal procedurally unfair. For this reason, an employer is well advised to keep a written record of any consideration which they give to bumping.

Notice

Employees who are made redundant must be given notice in accordance with their contract of employment.

The *statutory* minimum notice is:

One week's notice for employees who have been employed for at least a month but for less than 2 years;

Thereafter, a week's notice for every complete year employed up to a maximum of 12 years.

An employee's contract of employment might provide for a notice period longer than the statutory minimum, referred to as *contractual* notice, in which case it will be the period of contractual notice which applies.

The employment contract may also permit the employee to make a payment in lieu of notice. In the absence of a clause permitting a payment in lieu, to make such a payment would be a breach of the employment contract, at least in theory as such a claim is unlikely to be pursued in practice.

Appeals

Although the termination of employment by reason of redundancy is a dismissal, the *Acas Code of Practice on disciplinary and grievance procedures 2015* does not apply to dismissals due to redundancy. Therefore, an employer does not have to give an employee, dismissed for redundancy, a right to appeal.

However, the general advice is always to give an employee, chosen for redundancy, a right of appeal as if the Acas Code did apply. The reason is that an employment tribunal might view the employer's failure to give a right of appeal as evidence that the redundancy decision was subjective rather than objective, or otherwise view the redundancy procedure as generally flawed, resulting in an unfair dismissal.

Printed in Great Britain
by Amazon